I0842710

# A New Chapter

Joe and Michael were sitting in their living room, discussing a new project. Their lives were filled with creativity and adventure, traveling the world for their interior design business.

Despite their successful careers and travels, there was a certain void in their lives. They often wondered if they were ready to take the next step and start a family.

The phone rang, disrupting their usual afternoon workflow. The caller was from an adoption agency with the news that they were approved for adoption.

A wave of emotions rushed over them. They were thrilled and scared at the same time, unsure of how to react. After a moment of silence, they both agreed to meet the baby boy.

They were led to a room where
a small baby boy was sleeping
peacefully. The moment they laid
eyes on him, their hearts melted.
They knew he was the one.

They held the baby boy in
their arms, feeling a sense of
completeness. This was the missing
piece of their lives, the family they
always wanted.

They brought their baby boy home,
their lives changing in an instant.
Their home was no longer just a
house, it was a place filled with love
and joy.

They both committed to be the best
parents they could be, promising to
give their son a life full of love,
understanding, and happiness.

Their lives had taken a
beautiful turn. They continued to
work passionately, balancing their
careers with their responsibilities
as parents.

With each passing day, their love
for their son grew, watching him
laugh, learn, and grow. They knew
they had made the right decision.

They celebrated their son's first
birthday, a milestone that brought
immense joy to their lives. Their son
was growing up surrounded by love
and acceptance.

As they blew out the birthday
candles, they looked at each
other, grateful for the journey
they had undertaken. Their family
was complete, their love story,
a beautiful testament to their
journey.

The End.